KGA's Survival Guide for Managers

KGA's Survival Guide
for Managers

KATHLEEN GREER

Framingham, Massachusetts

2011

DEDICATION

KGA's Survival Guide for Managers is dedicated to the thousands of managers that we have supported over the years, our dedicated counselors, and the entire staff at KGA.

CONTENTS

Acknowledgments ix

Preface xi

1 Dealing with Troubled Employees 15

2 Having Difficult Conversations 27

3 Managing Counterproductive Behavior 32

4 Delivering Effective Performance Reviews 36

5 Managing Involuntary Separations 39

6 Receiving a Sexual Harassment Complaint 42

7 Handling a Workplace Violence Incident 50

8 Referring to an EAP 54

9 Managing the Stress of Managing 58

10 Leading Effective Meetings 62

11 Improving Employee Retention 65

12 Moving into a New Senior Role 68

ACKNOWLEDGMENTS

Many members of the KGA staff helped to write, edit, and proofread the individual chapters of *KGA's Survival Guide for Managers.* Special thanks go to Liz Hahn, Nancy Kerr, Katherine Orcutt, Monica Gibson, Elaine Varelas, Bob Cipriani, Ann Majkut, Carey Napoleone, Sue Penchansky, Dale Arsenault, Tyson Puetz, Chris Bouchard, Linda Piatelli, Karen Shaw, Lori Harrington, Michael McCourt, Carol Biebers, Jack Burke, Joseph Weintraub, James Hunt, Tyson Puetz, Ernie Kapopoulos, Betsy Pratt, Richard Emerson, Kristin Matthews, Laurel Fardella, Angela Carini, Liza Dunlay, Seth Moeller, Debbie Sarbacker, Sue Kapopoulos, and Nancy Mobley.

PREFACE

KGA's Survival Guide for Managers is based on nearly three decades of training, advising, and in-the-trenches problem solving. I believe deeply in the efficacy of Employee Assistance Programs.

The Survival Guide does not replace good training or a good EAP. But whether you have an EAP or not, the guide should be your "reach for" book. It is broken down into the day-to-day problems that haunt managers and hurt businesses. The ideal manager knows all this, knows everything about business, has a perfect family, does volunteer work, and leads a balanced life. I haven't met the ideal manager, and problems always arise when you are already stretched for time.

Read the book and know what it offers. When there is a problem, look it up and use the guide. It is designed to help you and reduce the stress of your job. If you have an EAP, it will supplement the program. If you don't have an EAP, it will outline the steps you need to resolve your concern.

The first three chapters of the Survival Guide address the tough issues related to managing troubled employees. They outline steps for having difficult conversations, managing counterproductive behavior, and intervening in deteriorating employee situations. The next two chapters cover the delivery of effective performance reviews and involuntary separations. Specific attention is given in chapters 6 and 7 to properly receiving sexual harassment complaints and preventing and addressing workplace violence incidents. Effective referrals to the EAP are the subject of the next chapter.

The final four chapters are dedicated to helping managers find the courage to grow and develop in their new roles. Chapter 9 is devoted to managing one's own stress due to work, including tools to help their employees with their stress. Chapter 10 addresses the basics of running a good meeting, a critical skill for a manager's success. Chapter 11 provides many tips for growing a team and improving employee retention. The final chapter is critical information for stepping into a new senior role.

Over the years, I have found that few business books address the challenges and anxieties that are commonly faced by managers. *KGA's Survival Guide* shares proven strategies for getting into the trenches and coming out a business leader.

KGA's Survival Guide for Managers

1.

DEALING WITH TROUBLED EMPLOYEES

The Employee Assistance Program (EAP) is an important resource that your company offers as a benefit to employees. As a supervisor or manager, your job may be easier because this service has been made available. Employees will have help available to them on a free and confidential basis when problems arise. You may wish to refer one of your employees to the EAP as part of your usual disciplinary procedures.

If you have an EAP in place, make sure that you understand how an employee takes advantage of it. Many employees look to you as a source of guidance and may want your opinion of the program. If it is presented positively, more people will take advantage of it. This is helpful to you as a manager because employees will seek help for minor issues instead of letting things fester, resulting in major job-related problems. Most personal problems do not go away when left untreated.

If you are unfamiliar with your company's EAP service, call the EAP to introduce yourself as a manager. Review the process for referring an employee and make sure your information is updated. If you have any reservations about the EAP after you make the call, discuss your concerns with Human

Resources. The EAP is one of your most powerful tools, and you have to feel completely confident in your program. There are variations in quality of EAPs and there is no reason that your company shouldn't have the best possible resource.

Job Performance

Job performance is the key to your role as a supervisor or manager. In your position, you have the responsibility to see that work gets done and that your employees do their jobs according to job standards.

You are in the unique position of knowing the job requirements of each person in your area, as well as being familiar with the past performance of each employee. When job performance declines, there may be several contributing factors. Sometimes poor job performance is the result of personal problems. Covering up or ignoring the situation helps no one. Suggest that the employee contact the EAP as soon as you suspect that a personal problem may be responsible for the job problem.

Intervention in the Workplace

We live in a world of stress. There is a lot of pressure on people to do more, earn more, be more. This pressure affects people differently. Everyone has a different manner of coping with stress and a different limit as to how much stress one can endure.

We all know that personally stressful situations occur, but we may not realize the frequency or the extent to which they affect people. It is estimated that one person in ten has an alcohol-related problem. Another one person in ten abuses drugs or a combination of drugs and alcohol. An additional two persons out of ten suffer at some time from an anxiety-related disorder or depression.

We also know the problems that can arise in the workplace when an employee is struggling with one of these difficulties. Attendance and performance suffer, as does the morale of those around the employee.

It takes tremendous courage for a person to admit that there is a problem and to decide to do something about it. Sometimes this step represents more of a burden than the person can handle and the situation is accepted as one more negative aspect of life. However, when someone else takes the first step by acknowledging the problem and offering to help, it eases that burden and makes it easier for the person to accept help.

So why don't we try harder to help people suffering from stress? Perhaps one reason is that sometimes it is easier to overlook another person's suffering. We rationalize the obvious signs of internal distress because it is none of our business. We don't want to hurt the person's feelings; we don't want to pry; we don't want to violate someone's rights; we don't want to make unjustified accusations. There comes a time, however, when someone must make the first move. This move is called *intervention*.

Whose Responsibility Is It to Intervene?

Intervention is appropriate when someone is having a problem that prevents normal functioning. Techniques and suggestions will be covered in detail later, but for now, know that intervention requires sensitivity, tact, firmness, and the confidence that you are doing the right thing. If you feel that someone is having a problem, then intervention is in the employee's best interest.

To intervene, you do not have to pinpoint what is causing the person's problem. That is the responsibility of the EAP counselor or another professional person. You only need to recognize that someone has a problem and to be committed to helping that employee find help.

Anyone, including friends and coworkers, who observes that someone needs help can intervene. However, in the workplace, the final responsibility usually falls to the employee's immediate supervisor or manager.

If you don't feel comfortable making this evaluation or speaking to the person, consider calling your EAP for feedback, guidance, and moral support along the way. An EAP counselor has experience in dealing with employees with difficulties and can help you identify whether there may be a problem, and help you decide how to handle it. The counselor can also take an active part in the intervention process.

How to Recognize a Problem

The problems or disorders that can adversely affect someone's performance are varied, but often manifest themselves in similar ways. Here is a list of signs that you might notice in a co-worker who is experiencing one of these problems. (Note that many of us display some of these symptoms at one time or another. They become abnormal when they are both chronic and out of character.) As you read through this list, ask yourself if the questions that follow apply to a problem employee.

Absenteeism

Is the employee absent often, particularly on Mondays or on Friday afternoons? This is often a way to extend the weekend.

Tardiness

Is the employee often late arriving in the morning or returning after lunch? An inability to get going in the morning or to be on time is a type of resistance that has many sources.

Gaps in the day

Are there periods in the day when the employee disappears and is nowhere to be found? Does the employee take frequent, long coffee breaks?

Oversensitivity

Does the employee seem to take everything the wrong way or overreact to criticism? Does the employee respond negatively where no offense is intended?

Defensiveness

Does the employee always feel that people are working against him/her, or interpret general criticism as being directed toward oneself?

Mood swings/erratic behavior

Does the employee's mood fluctuate from being very happy to very somber? Is the employee sometimes abnormally outgoing or loud?

Lack of concentration

Does the employee frequently lose track of a conversation? Does the employee have difficulty thinking through a sequence of thoughts or steps?

Inability to complete a task or make a decision

Are there often loose ends or abandoned tasks? Is the employee indecisive or contradictory when asked for a definite answer?

Impaired performance

Is the quality or quantity of the employee's work significantly less than usual?

Difficulty working with others

Does the employee find it difficult to maintain a working

relationship with others? Do others find it difficult to work with the employee because they have to compensate for the person's behavior?

Types of Problems

The previous issues are symptomatic of a variety of disorders, including chemical dependence, alcoholism, and other stress-related problems. The employee could be having serious marital, financial, or health problems, or could be responding to pressure from a combination of sources, or suffering from depression.

Again, it is not the manager's responsibility to determine the cause of the problem, but merely to recognize the need for help. Intervention before a crisis helps the employee to seek treatment at an early stage and may help the company save a valuable employee.

Your Role as a Supervisor or Manager

As a supervisor or manager, your expertise lies in the area of job performance. You are not a trained counselor and should not attempt to assess problems or counsel employees. The Employee Assistance Program can be your most effective management tool.

When faced with an employee's declining job performance, feelings sometimes get in the way of taking an appropriate action. You may feel guilty about the problem, as if you are responsible for the employee's failure. You may feel let down or disappointed because of high expectations. You may get angry because the employee's poor performance reflects on your ability to get work done. All of these feelings are normal, but may prevent an appropriate action from taking place. Try to look at your feelings before confronting the employee.

As a supervisor or manager, you are not immune to personal problems. You may find that handling a troubled employee triggers feelings in you that are difficult to manage. You also may develop a problem in your personal life which requires attention. In any case, remember that the EAP is available for you, as well as for the employees you supervise. All personal contact with the program will be held in the strictest confidence.

How to Approach Someone

Intervention should be done in a non-intimidating manner. This is difficult because usually, at the time of intervention, the problem is serious enough that the person's job performance is suffering.

Before you meet with the employee, it would be helpful to follow these steps. (Remember that the EAP counselor can help you with this process.) These steps apply for peer intervention as well as manager/employee intervention.

Observe the Employee Objectively

List the issues as you see them

This list should contain specific incidents, behavior, or observations, not generalizations or conclusions.

Discuss the situation

Before you meet, identify what you want to accomplish with the employee. Try to anticipate all possible responses. (Be prepared to deal with denial.) Consider, for example, how you will respond if the employee refuses to cooperate or tells you that everything will work itself out in time.

Do not analyze the cause

Remember that your goal is not to analyze the root of the problem, but to recognize that it exists, and determine what further action should be taken. Tell the person your concerns. Emphasize that you want to help. List the things that you have observed, and tell how these incidents affected you and your work. State how you feel as a result of these things. Then tell the person that you need help resolving the problem and that you have to come up with a plan to prevent these things from continuing.

Come up with a plan

Determine which of your available resources seem appropriate for this situation. Perhaps the employee will be able to offer suggestions.

Plan a follow-up meeting after a specific interval

This important step can afford the employee an opportunity to inform the manager of any progress in meeting established goals, and to be certain that both parties agree that positive action is happening.

Other Suggestions

♦ Take time to establish a relationship with each employee.

♦ Keep a record of every employee's work performance documenting both the positive and negative.

♦ If you are unsure about how to proceed, contact your own manager, your human resources department, or the employee assistance consultant for advice.

♦ Don't delay. The sooner you take action, the sooner the employee can get help.

♦ Have an informal talk. Tell the employee that job performance is below standards.

♦ If it appears that the declining job performance is a result of a personal problem, suggest that the employee contact the EAP for a confidential appointment.

♦ Don't moralize or discuss the problem with the employee. Make clear what the employee must do to meet expectations. Be consistent and clear about your job standards. Make a plan to meet with the employee to review performance and follow through with this plan.

♦ Emphasize that the EAP program is confidential and that initial sessions are paid for by the company.

♦ Be aware that if the employee gives written permission, the EAP will inform you about the employee's willingness to follow through with recommendations. The EAP consultant will not discuss the employee's problem with you.

Guidelines

When you meet with the employee, try to be non-threatening so as to facilitate and communicate, but, at the same time, maintain control of the session.

Some guidelines for the session are:

♦ Stick to specific incidents and behavioral observations because they are less open to interpretation.

♦ Beware of excuses and denial on the part of the employee. Excuses can be an extension of the underlying problem. Maintain your assertiveness.

♦ Compromises are not solutions. They only delay reaching a solution and give the employee control of the situation.

♦ Goals should be measurable, attainable by the employee, and acceptable to the employer.

Remember...

Approximately four people out of ten experience problems that affect their job performance at one time or another. Only about one out of ten is helped through an employee assistance program. Sometimes people recognize their problems and seek help on their own. Unchecked, these problems can get beyond their control.

An employee can lose a job or can become a problem to the company. Through the intervention process described above, the employee can get help and probably return to the previous level of functioning.

Remember, too, that intervention makes smart business sense. After all, businesses invest a lot of money in recruiting, training, and benefits programs. It is much more cost-effective to help a valuable person overcome an obstacle than to duplicate that investment and lose the benefit of the employee's experience.

2.

HAVING DIFFICULT CONVERSATIONS

One of the most stressful parts of a manager's job is to initiate and carry out a difficult conversation with an employee. These are the conversations that often keep managers up at night, ruminating about what to say and how to say it. The conversation may involve confronting an employee about poor performance, a difficult decision, an upcoming disciplinary action, or confronting some type of counterproductive behavior. Whatever the subject, preparation may help to alleviate the stress associated with these conversations.

"The earlier the better" is the best advice on timing when it comes to having a difficult conversation. Most managers tend to procrastinate, hoping the situation will go away or just get better with time. And, almost two-thirds of the time, things do improve; but what about the other third?

Regardless of all the preparations, the conversation may still be difficult to initiate and carry out, simply because having them is difficult for most people. Knowing that you are well prepared for the conversation will make it better, at least to some extent.

Employees who have personal issues that are not improving—such as substance abuse, financial stress, or relationship stress—will often show a decline in work performance. Most counterproductive behavior such as "stirring the pot" or other acting out at work will not improve without intervention.

Without a manager intervention, difficult employees may get more difficult, affecting the morale of the whole group. The best thing a manager or supervisor can do is to give feedback just as soon as a noticeable performance issue emerges.

Step 1: Initiate a conversation

Some suggested phrases:

"We need to have a difficult conversation."

"I have noticed some decline in your... (work performance, productivity, attendance, etc.)"

"I know that you are going through some personal issues and I want to be sensitive to that; however, it is starting to affect the... (morale of others, quality of your work, opinion of senior management.)"

"I am interested in helping you get back on track."

Step 2: Describe the behavior

Clarify what you have observed, and remind the employee what improvement is needed:

"I have noticed you disappearing for long periods of time during the work day, and I need you to be available."

"I am aware that you are bad-mouthing me behind my back and I need you to stop."

"You don't seem prepared for meetings, and I need you to come with solutions and documentation."

"I've noticed that you seem unhappy lately, and I want to talk to you about it."

Step 3: Refer to the EAP if necessary

If during the conversation it appears that some personal problems are the root cause, talk directly about the availability of the EAP:

"Have you thought about talking to a professional about your situation?

"Are you aware that we have an EAP?"

"Do you know how to get in touch with the EAP?"

Step 4: Follow-up and document

Agree on a short time frame, such as two weeks, to have a second conversation. At that time, follow up with the employee to check in on what has changed:

"I've noticed that your work performance . . . (has improved, is about the same) . . . since we talked."

"Were you able to connect with the EAP?"

"I am concerned that if there isn't improvement soon, I will be forced to give you a written warning. That is the first step in progressive discipline, and I am still hoping we can avoid taking that action."

Other suggestions for difficult conversations:

+ Be prepared by thinking things through, making notes, and practicing the conversation in front of a mirror or with a trusted advisor.

+ Remember that your view of the situation may be one-sided and be prepared to hear a different point of view.

+ Think about what is at stake and what an ideal outcome might look like.

+ Practice stress-reduction techniques such as breathing exercises that you can use before, during, and after the conversation.

+ Try to put yourself in the other person's shoes, empathizing with his or her feelings.

+ Take responsibility for how you may have contributed to the situation.

+ Re-state a description of the problem and the proposed solution to see if there is some agreement.

• Follow up with an email that will serve as documentation of the conversation and proposed actions.

Helping to turn around a declining work situation is one of the most rewarding experiences in a manager or supervisor's life. If you have been putting off a difficult conversation, now is the time.

3.
MANAGING COUNTERPRODUCTIVE BEHAVIOR

Counterproductive behaviors are those behaviors that tend to work against one's success in an organization. They may be mild or severe, chronic or acute. The role of the manager is to notice the behavior and proactively respond to it as soon as possible. If the person behaving negatively is your employee, letting these behaviors fester can damage your reputation and that of your employee.

What are some examples of counterproductive behavior in the workplace?

- Bullying

- Back-stabbing

- Shouting

- Acting out

- Showing favoritism

+ Ostracizing someone

+ Displaying negativity

+ Stirring the pot

+ Rumor spreading

+ Taking advantage of someone

+ Not listening

+ Complaining

+ Withdrawing

+ Not getting along with people

Does this remind you of high school? Unfortunately, most counterproductive behavior could be labeled as "immature" behavior as well. Often people who display counterproductive behavior are intelligent and competent, but fall back on old patterns without thinking. They may lack emotional intelligence and maturity.

They may have come from a family where these types of behaviors were common, or from a work environment where high-school-like behavior was tolerated. Perhaps there is an underlying personal problem and these behaviors are employed as a coping mechanism. Whatever the reason, the manager's role is to notice it, provide feedback, and set appropriate limits to extinguish the behavior as soon as possible.

When you notice counterproductive behavior, follow the five-step formula:

Step 1: Recognize the problem

Recognize the problem. Don't turn your back on it.

Step 2: Document examples

Document examples to help you in your discussion.

Step 3: Discuss performance

Explain how the employee's behavior has impacted you or others and how it could affect co-workers if it continues.

Step 4: Consider a referral

Consider referral to the EAP. As a manager, or supervisor, you can call the EAP to discuss your situation. Since there may be personal issues affecting the employee, be sure to mention the availability of the EAP for confidential counseling.

Step 5: Monitor progress and provide feedback

Monitor progress and provide feedback. Be consistent in your feedback until the behavior is extinguished.

Once the counterproductive behavior is eliminated, the employee may not be "home free." Some damage may have been done in terms of group cohesiveness.

If the employee is a manager of a group, team morale and performance or interpersonal communications may have been affected. An employee may, upon facing the reality of the impact of his or her counterproductive behavior, realize the need for individualized coaching for more long-term permanent results.

Although confronting problem behavior is one of the more difficult manager tasks, the rewards can be great. Seeing a difficult employee become a productive employee can be a very gratifying supervisory experience.

4.

DELIVERING EFFECTIVE PERFORMANCE REVIEWS

Performance reviews are often dreaded by managers and therefore are avoided. "I just haven't had time," "He knows how he's doing," or "I'll get it next quarter," are common excuses. When feedback is given regularly, performance reviews are no problem at all. Everyone knows where the employee stands, and expectations are clear.

Here are ten suggestions for more effective performance reviews.

Start early

> There should be no surprises in a review because you've been giving feedback all along, positive and negative. Ask for status reports on a regular basis to avoid getting off track.

Plan carefully

> Performance reviews are incredibly important to employees. Stick to a scheduled appointment and give it a

priority. Meet in a private place and don't allow interruptions during the review.

Bring along documentation

It will be helpful to refer to a copy of the job description, project lists and other pertinent information. Think ahead of the meeting about what a good outcome would be if everything goes well.

Don't get hung up on forms

Lots of managers agonize over what form to use and end up skipping the review completely. An effective review can just be a good discussion about what went well, what didn't, areas for improvement, and areas for development. Development activities might include coaching, cross training, education, or special project opportunities.

Tie in the big picture

It always helps to know how you fit in. Use the opportunity to tie the employee's job to the goals of the department and the organization.

Be specific

Whether giving positive or negative feedback, have meaningful examples at hand. This will show that you've been paying attention and are prepared for the meeting.

Put the person at ease

Reviews are nerve-racking for most employees. Use your best listening skills and empathy to create an open environment and watch for "coachable moments."

Keep quiet

Give the employee plenty of time to talk. You may have been missing valuable feedback from your employee during your busy days.

Tie the review to compensation

Even if salary freezes are holding you back, you still may be able to give a spot bonus to someone who has been exemplary. At the very least, a gift card for a night out sends a message that you appreciate someone's work.

Start documenting

Make a vow with yourself to keep a better handle on managing performance and performance reviews. Put reminders in your calendar for monthly or quarterly meetings to communicate about progress and performance. Remember, managing performance is a process, not an event.

5.
MANAGING INVOLUNTARY
SEPARATIONS

One of those most difficult of conversations is the one that takes place when employment is being terminated, either for cause or because of a reduction in force. The loss of employment is traumatic for the manager, as well as the employee, regardless of the circumstances. The best advice for managers is to put yourself in their position and ask yourself how you would want to be treated.

Get centered

Take a few minutes of quiet time for yourself to get centered. Practicing some simple breathing exercises can calm you and help you to think clearly.

Prepare your remarks

Prepare what you are going to say prior to meeting with the employee. Refrain from debating the event.

A calm demeanor and prepared delivery will help you and the employee through a difficult time.

Avoid small talk

Prolonging the news of a termination will not make it any easier. Try to avoid the temptation to cushion the blow by talking about the weather or inquiring about one's family.

Be direct

Avoid giving mixed messages that may confuse the employee as to why they are being terminated from the company. Be prepared to repeat your news and instructions more than once as it starts to sink in.

Let the employee vent

There may be silence, tears, or anger at the meeting. Sitting with those emotions will make it easier for everyone to move on. Some managers rush the process for their own benefit because of their own discomfort.

Respect dignity

If there are no anticipated security issues, allow terminated employees to return to their cubes to say goodbye to friends and coworkers. This will help to avoid the embarrassment of being escorted from the building and will help employees deal with loss.

Be honest

There may be nothing you can say to alleviate the pain

of this situation. As awkward as it is, sitting with someone's grief may be all that you can do. Acknowledging how difficult the situation is may be helpful.

When an organization executes a well-planned separation, it should be as humanistic as possible. If circumstances warrant, providing severance pay, outplacement assistance, and extending EAP services can help the employee find future opportunities. If managers can help affected employees maintain a sense of dignity, everyone will benefit.

6.

RECEIVING A SEXUAL HARASSMENT COMPLAINT

Most mid- to large-sized companies have policies in place to deal with sexual harassment. In some states, laws have been enacted to require dissemination of the policies to employees on an annual basis.

Many companies have established sexual harassment prevention training programs to help support state and federal guidelines. These programs also help to create a corporate culture that is free of harassment where people can focus on doing their jobs without needing to worry about being harassed. Check with your state to clarify the requirement. Always include Human Resources in harassment complaints.

Although policies are in place to prevent harassment, managers often are not sure what to do in the first meeting with an employee who brings forward a complaint. This is typical of what happens when someone approaches a manager with a sexual harassment complaint. The complaint may be brought to you at the worst possible time, usually when you least expect it. How you react will set the tone for the events that follow. What do you say? What do you do?

How do you avoid the most common mistakes that managers make during the first meeting?

The Anxiety of the First Meeting

When a victim of harassment comes forward, he or she has usually spent days, weeks, or months debating whether to bring the issue to your attention. More than 90% of the people who experience harassment decide not to make a formal complaint because of the perceived risk involved.

"Things are bad now but will they be worse afterward?"

"I am too embarrassed by what happened to let anyone know about it."

"What will it do to my career?"

"Will my boss believe me?"

"What if there is retaliation after I complain?"

Anxiety builds as the employee makes the decision to take a risk and bring the complaint forward. Out of a variety of options, the victim has chosen *you* to be the first one to know about the complaint. The pressure is on.

Managers and supervisors may or may not be trained in sexual harassment laws. Many are aware that the Civil Rights Act of 1991 made it easy for victims to go to court, and that, in addition to corporate liability, some managers and supervisors have been held personally liable. Even managers and supervisors with little training know that a sexual harassment complaint is not something to take lightly. So the anxiety builds for all involved.

Goals of the First Meeting

The overall goal of the first meeting is to prevent the situation from deteriorating before action can be taken by helping the employee feel that coming forward was the right thing to do. This can be accomplished by taking a number of steps that put the employee at ease while being decisive, supportive, and reassuring. The goal has been reached when the employee leaves the first meeting feeling glad that he or she came forward with the complaint.

Strategies During the First Meeting

Schedule

Once you determine the nature of the complaint, you must evaluate your time to determine whether you can give undivided attention. If you cannot get out of the meeting across town, schedule an hour for later that day. "I am really glad that you are bringing this to my attention. Unfortunately, I cannot cancel this meeting but would like to meet with you today to give this matter the attention it deserves. Could we meet at 2:00?"

Minimize distraction

When the meeting does take place, give the complainant

your complete attention. Hold the meeting in an office setting, sit in a non-intimidating manner, and hold all calls.

Ask open ended questions

Even the most assertive person may be thrown off when victimized by sexual harassment. Ask the person to describe the history and sequence of events. "What happened? Tell me about.... Describe for me.... Could you give some examples of...." Restate and ask questions to clarify information, but don't overdo it. The details can be sifted through later during an investigation.

Listen well

Focus on what the person is saying. Take notes, watch for discomfort, and give the victim time to speak. Keeping quiet while the person tells the story is important. If the victim is having a very difficult time talking to you and if there is a gender difference between you and the victim, you may consider referring the employee to an appropriate person of the same gender. Ask whether he or she can talk with you or needs someone else. Do not be too quick, however, to pass the person off, since they have chosen you out of a variety of possibilities.

Be supportive yet neutral

It is important to balance support and empathy with fact

finding. Help the victim feel that he or she has done the right thing by bringing the matter to your attention. "I am very sorry that you are going through this. I am really glad that you came to talk to me. We take these matters very seriously and I want to help to resolve the situation." These statements of support do not imply that you necessarily believe or agree with the victim.

Determine the desired outcomes

Ask the victim what he or she needs to feel comfortable at work again. Avoid asking, "What would you like to have happen?" as this implies that the recipient has some influence over the disciplinary decisions. Focus on the desired outcome for the recipient.

Pledges of confidentiality

Managers are often put in the difficult position of having an employee ask for complete confidentiality. "I would like to tell you about something that happened to me, but I want to make sure that if I do that it can stay just between us." Do not fall into that trap with a harassment complaint. Once you know about something, it is the same as the company knowing, and you probably have a policy that dictates who in the company needs to know about the complaint. What you can promise to employees is that you will keep the "circle" as small as possible after a complaint is brought forward.

Inform about next steps

It is reassuring at this stage to hear something about what will happen after the meeting

"After you leave, I am going to call Sue Jones in Human Resources. Within a day or so, she will get in touch with you to hear your situation in little more detail. It would be helpful if you made some notes for yourself to go over with Sue. After you talk with Sue, she will probably want to talk with the person about whom you have lodged the complaint, and perhaps several witnesses. Within a week or so, Sue and I will meet with you to further discuss what the situation. In the meantime, is there anything I can do to make you more comfortable at work?"

Be reassuring about the victim's job status.

Obtain consultation from human resources

Review your own policy on harassment complaints and turn to the appropriate experts in your company. Even minor complaints handled at the lowest level should be brought to the attention of Human Resources. Human Resources may be aware of prior complaints about the same person, or they may have suggestions for diffusing the anxiety in the department.

Document

Document all of your discussions with the victim and with Human Resources. Should a case end up in court or with a state discrimination agency, they generally look for whether you knew or should have known about a situation, and whether you took immediate and appropriate action. Documentation is one good safeguard for showing that you did all the right things.

The Three Tests of Harassment

There are at least three considerations when deciding whether a behavior might constitute harassment. Looking at an incident in different ways may help clear up the perceptions in a difficult situation.

1. Was the behavior welcome?

In general, welcome behavior is not sexual harassment. An exception might be in the cases of "non-participants," where people have been offended by something that was not deliberately intended for them.

2. Is this a repetitive or pervasive behavior

Most sexual harassment cases involve repeated or pervasive behavior of a sexual nature. An exception might be a case where the behavior was so offensive or destructive that it did not need to be repeated in order to result in serious disciplinary action.

3. Is the victim's perception reasonable?

Most juries are instructed to try to "think like a reasonable person" in deciding sexual harassment cases. If you do not agree with someone else's perception, try imaging yourself as a reasonable juror assigned to decide on the case.

New Perspectives on Sexual Harassment

If you are having difficulty deciding whether something is reasonable, it can be helpful to relate it to your own values or attitudes. These three questions may be helpful in gaining perspective on sexual harassment:

How would you feel about being quoted or pictured in the company newsletter?

How would you feel if your mother, daughter, father, or partner were able to observe your behavior?

What would you do differently if the third graders from the local public school were visiting the workplace and observed what was taking place?

Summary

Harassment is a difficult subject because it involves perception, cultural issues, and the personal limits of each person involved. Avoid getting caught up in determining guilt or innocence during the first meeting or in saying something that may be perceived as "blaming the victim." Your job in the first meeting is to make certain the employee leaves feeling that he or she has made the right decision in coming forward. With that accomplished, you can turn to the experts for assistance.

7.

HANDLING A WORKPLACE VIOLENCE INCIDENT

The Occupational Safety and Health Act (OSHA) defines workplace violence as violence or the threat of violence against workers. It can occur at or outside the workplace and can range from threats and verbal abuse to physical assaults and homicide, one of the leading causes of job-related deaths. Workplace violence is a growing concern for employers and employees alike. The odds of having a critical incident occur in your workplace are greater than you may think and no workplace is immune.

Consider the following possibilities:

+ Serious injury, accident or death

+ Physical fighting or other violence

+ Suicide

+ Fighting or other threats of Domestic violence

+ Armed robbery

- Sexual assault

- Mentally disturbed behavior from employees or others

As a people manager, you never know when you will need to respond to a critical incident of workplace violence affecting your organization. There are actions you can take in advance of a situation occurring to prepare you for an event during a time of high stress and crisis.

Become familiar with your company's workplace violence policy and the available resources in place to help you in the event of a situation occurring. If a policy does not exist, speak with your leadership team to develop a policy and response protocol.

Ensure your employees are aware of the policy, that they understand there is zero tolerance for violent behavior within the workplace, and that any and all reports of such violence will be addressed swiftly.

Make certain all employees are aware of the emergency response protocol and any particular role they need to play in the event of an emergency.

If an incident happens in the workplace:

Implement your organization's emergency response protocol

Check to be sure people are safe

Debrief the organization

Following a major crisis in the workplace, it is important to debrief the organization within a 24 to 36 hour period. The EAP is available 24/7 to help you plan your response.

Notify the EAP

Notify the EAP so they can be available to help employees understand some of the reactions they may be experiencing.

Sometimes people are unclear about how to respond to a workplace tragedy and struggle with knowing what to do. Having resources available to help them talk through their feelings is a critical element in the healing process.

A follow-up debriefing within a couple of weeks, with the same EAP resource, provides an opportunity to engage with employees and to get a sense of where they are in the healing process. This creates an environment for employees to share what coping strategies have worked for them and to further discuss feelings which may have surfaced in the interim.

As the manager of the impacted group, it is important for you to keep a pulse on the organization and stay alert for any signs of employee distress or shifts in behavior. It can take some individuals a period of time to fully comprehend such an event. In addition to your usual communication and interaction with employees, be sure to reach-out to any employee you feel may benefit from a more personal connection.

If you believe the employee could benefit from one-on-one counseling, provide the necessary contact information for the EAP.

The role of manager is pivotal on a day-to-day basis and even more so in the face of a tragedy or crisis. Take care of yourself. Your leadership has never been more important to your team. Don't go it alone. Seek out the help you may need for yourself as the burden you are shouldering is heavy. You can best help others by taking care of yourself.

Keep lines of communication open, and ensure you have an environment where employees feel safe sharing their feelings and concerns about the situation.

Talk with Human Resources about developing a training program to help employees recognize the signs of potential workplace violence. This is a proactive prevention strategy.

8.

REFERRING TO AN EAP

There are many signs and symptoms that alert a manager to the need for employee counseling. An EAP referral often makes sense, instead of trying to help an employee with his or her personal issues. The need may become apparent after a serious workplace issue such as sexual harassment or violence. However, most often, referrals are needed when a personal issue of some type affects the performance of an employee or distress becomes visible. The EAP can be a great resource in these circumstances.

The EAP can provide consultation to the manager, as well as direct counseling for the employee. The EAP may provide short-term counseling or a referral for psychotherapy. Employee Assistance Programs generally have expertise in all types of relationship issues, anxiety and depression, and work life balance. Some EAPs can also help with confidential child and eldercare referrals, financial and legal consultation, career counseling, and wellness coaching.

A good first step for a manager is to call the EAP to discuss the situation. This gives the manager a chance to sort out what has been happening and get some initial consultation about how to approach an employee. Most manager referrals to the EAP are informal with the manager simply commenting on the employee's behavior change and reminding him about the EAP as a resource.

The supervisory referral process is a service offered by the EAP for managers and employees to utilize when the employee's problem becomes a problem to the workplace as well. The formal supervisory referral is initiated by a manager or HR professional, but always with the knowledge of HR. Human Resources Departments know company policies, may be able to help with coaching and avoiding legal issues, and often have additional information about a situation. Some companies do not use supervisory referrals at all, so managers must always check with HR before initiating a supervisory referral with the EAP.

A formal supervisory referral is made because an employee has displayed behaviors that are interfering with job performance. In these cases, the employer has an investment in the employee and wants to support the employee to get back on track. The referral includes an assessment, referral, and if recommended, case management of treatment offered to the employee.

An example may be an employee who is showing signs of alcohol or substance abuse, or perhaps someone whose emotional or behavioral issues impact job performance.

The EAP acts as a liaison between the company, the employee, and the treating facility. With a release of information signed by the employee, a representative from the EAP notifies the employer that the employee is complying with or is not complying with recommended mental health or substance abuse treatment.

Here are some considerations for managers before initiating a supervisory referral:

♦ Employees get back on track sooner when managers take early action on performance issues. This is true when there is an interfering personal problem as well.

♦ A supervisory referral may be formal or informal. In both cases, a referral to the EAP may be the most helpful action to take with a troubled employee.

♦ An informal supervisory referral occurs when a manager mentions the availability of the EAP to an employee. Examples of these referrals include a manager saying, "Are you aware that we have an EAP?" or, "Have you thought about calling the EAP to get some help for your problem?"

♦ A formal supervisory referral occurs when there is a documented performance issue and disciplinary action is in process. The employee must be made aware of this process from the beginning.

♦ Few supervisory referrals are mandatory. Mandatory referrals must be supported by a strong company policy and are only used when there are safety sensitive situations. In most cases, managers may "strongly suggest" the EAP during progressive discipline, but it is always the employee's choice as to whether or not he/she avails him/herself of help through the EAP.

It is strongly suggested that a manager call the EAP with a

heads-up before referring the employee to the EAP in a formal supervisory referral. It gives the EAP and manager an opportunity to discuss the case and plan next steps. For example, the manager can be coached on how to talk with the employee about signing a release of information.

Partnering with an EAP on a successful referral to the EAP can be one of the most gratifying events in a manager's professional life. There is really nothing more rewarding than connecting an employee with the right help at the right time. Managers have the opportunity to prevent a problem from becoming bigger, or perhaps even save a life, by referring employees to appropriate help.

9.

MANAGING THE STRESS OF MANAGING

Why should I pay attention to Stress Management?

Managers and supervisors can make a big difference in the lives of their employees. You may help get a person back on track after a crisis or help someone live a happier and well balanced life.

There can be tremendous satisfaction in the *people* side of management. Stress can cause severe performance problems at work, ultimately impacting the productivity of an organization. Learning about stress management may help you, your employees, and the company at the same time.

Remember that by practicing good stress management and keeping a balanced life style, you are setting a good example for your work group.

What do I need to know about Stress Management?

Stress affects everyone differently. Some people handle change better and are more resilient than others. Try to listen to and understand each employee and avoid judgment.

Most people want to do a good job and expect some work pressure. But too much pressure can lead to a vicious cycle of stress: poor performance ... declining confidence ... worse performance.

When a stress-related problem develops, ask yourself what type of employee you have. Is this someone who is generally a good performer or someone who is always difficult? This may determine how you support this employee and how long you can expect their performance to be affected.

Keep in mind that change is traumatic for some employees. Previous change or trauma may cause an extreme reaction to a current work situation. Poor performance may be a temporary situation while they adjust to this new change.

Employees often become unreasonable during times of change. You can help them by sharing information and listening to their concerns. Ask yourself if there is any way to make your workplace more enjoyable during a difficult time of prolonged stress.

Extreme stress such as divorce, death of a loved one, illness, or war may cause extreme stress symptoms. It is okay to make temporary adjustments for someone who has extreme stress, but generally expect some improvement in 6-8 weeks. You can end up doing someone more harm than good if you let them "slack off" for too long.

What should I tell employees about stress management?

Show that you take stress management seriously. Left ignored, stress can have debilitating effects on the health, welfare, and productivity of employees.

Provide stress management education for all your employees. Make sure that you know all of what they are learning. This will give everyone a common language. Use this as a springboard for implementing specific techniques at the work site. Ask employees for suggestions.

Remind employees to practice good stress management including physical exercise and good nutrition. Remember: what you do to manage your own stress sends a strong message to employees.

How can a manager or supervisor make a difference?

Effective Time Management may be one of the best ways to alleviate stress in your work group.

Demonstrating your skills in this area is the first step. Help employees get organized, prioritize goals and tasks, and keep a daily to-do list.

Nurture a workplace environment that demonstrates to employees that you care about their wellbeing.

During stressful times, make sure people understand the changes that are taking place and the requirements of their job. "Big picture" knowledge may help them see where the changes fit in.

Uncertainty about job security causes a lot of stress for

employees. Whenever possible, communicate well and often about the future.

The leading causes of stress at work result from poor communication, lack of feedback, and comments that make one feel undervalued. If you are unsure whether you are causing unneeded stress, find ways to solicit feedback from your employees either directly or indirectly.

Establish effective communication within your work group, through formal and informal methods, to ensure that you and your employees have a clear understanding of workplace issues and processes.

Clearly define priorities, for both yourself and your employees. Clearly define roles so that people know who is responsible for various workplace activities and understand decision-making latitude.

Establish ways for employees with legitimate concerns about safety or productivity to be heard.

Become a partner with, and promote, your Employee Assistance Program. The EAP is a free, confidential resource for all employees, providing counseling services and help for numerous work/life matters.

10.

LEADING EFFECTIVE MEETINGS

With all the time spent in meetings, it is well worth the effort to streamline meetings in order to make them more effective. As a manager, it is critical that you take a leadership role in making meetings run more efficiently in your organization. The best way to do this is to enlist the help of your entire group. These are some guidelines that apply to facilitators, attendees, and scribes.

For Facilitators

Ask for agenda

Ask for agenda items and time allowances at least 24 hours in advance so you can organize the agenda. If participants need to be present for certain items, schedule them at the beginning of the meeting or at a specific time. Check to see if people will be calling in so you can email them all of the materials in advance.

Bring all of your reference materials

Consider how to help "quiet" people participate and "talkers" to share the time equally with others. Include remote callers in the conversation.

Start on time and end on time

Leave 5 minutes to debrief at the end. Ask for feedback about how the meeting could have gone better. Agree on future meeting times. Make sure that all projects and tasks are assigned and expectations are clear. Create a list of unassigned projects to track.

For Attendees

Post ground rules

Post ground rules that can be referred to during the meeting. Help to make each meeting a positive and professional experience. Everyone can help the meeting stay on topic. A topic that involves a limited number of people should be addressed with a side meeting instead of trying to fit it into a bigger meeting for "efficiency." Show up on time and pay attention during the meeting. Avoid reading email in meetings. Keep PDAs on buzzer and leave the room if you have to respond to a critical phone call. Avoid side conversations. Take notes and make contributions when possible.

Bring all of your reference materials

Bring reference materials to the meeting. At the end, join in debriefing the meeting. Share comments about the meeting to avoid doing it later in a "behind closed doors" manner. After the meeting, complete all quick actions (less than 5 minutes) right away. Add the others to your to-do list or project list.

For Scribes

Highlight key issues, action items, and completion dates

Highlight key issues, action items, and completion dates that were agreed to in the meeting. Record who is accountable for each project. Distribute the minutes within two days of the meeting, in email format.

Once you gain consensus about some new rules for effective meetings, you may find that some employees need extra coaching or training in these skills. It is well worth the time and/or money to help every member of the group improve meeting management skills.

11.
IMPROVING EMPLOYEE RETENTION

It is difficult to keep employees motivated during economic downturns. Benefits and perks are reduced, and many employees take a "wait and see" attitude toward their jobs. Attrition is low, but commitment may be more of a financial matter than a true measure of engagement.

During times when the job market is strong, managers are faced with a real need to retain healthy and productive employees. An organization that has an engaged workforce benefits from employees who are proactive and actively contribute to the strategic and operational goals of the company. Research shows there is a strong correlation between an engaged workforce, strong customer satisfaction, and healthy financial performance.

How do you know if you have an engaged workforce?

Employees are energized by the work and the work environment.

The work environment encourages employees to "be yourself," which is a strong motivational factor.

Employees are receptive to new ideas and ways of doing things, listen actively and offer support and challenges because they care about the results.

Employees are proactive, involved in the process, and are not behaving as bystanders. Employees feel ownership for the outcomes.

There are visible high achievers who show company pride.

What can you do to improve employee engagement?

Establish clear accountability for success.

Employee engagement must be a part of every manager's performance goals and objectives.

Every employee needs to understand the importance your organization puts on employee engagement, what your employee engagement plan is, and how it will be measured.

Track your own progress and celebrate your successes.

Believe in what you do, it will bring results. If you don't believe in what you do, you can't expect your employees to believe in it either.

Be honest, and others will be honest in return.

Praise people and "catch them" doing something right. Say "Thank you."

Take an interest in your employees; spend a minute to have a chat. Ask how their family is doing, how they are doing, and ask if they are happy with their work.

Listen and learn from your employees.

Communicate clearly so employees know what needs to be done and what is expected of them.

Support your employees. Help them be successful and achieve the desired results.

Create a positive and open environment where employees feel valued, safe, and are equally comfortable bringing forward solutions as well as problems.

12.

MOVING INTO A NEW SENIOR ROLE

One of the most difficult challenges that a manager faces is being promoted into a more senior role. People are watching you and trying to determine if you are up to the challenge. They are comparing you to past leaders and wondering if you have what it takes to be successful. Do you have the tools to face this new position?

A Broader Scope

Most likely, your new role is broader in scope and you are now looking across a larger span of responsibility than before. Your sphere of influence is wider, broader, deeper. There are more decisions to be made more quickly and with less information.

Internal politics are more apparent and agendas and conflicts begin to surface. Strategies and plans can be easily derailed, and building relationships become critical to your success. You need to determine what success means for you in this new role both professionally and personally.

Broader Focus

To be successful, you need to be vigilant on many levels. You will learn to:

* Focus on the "big picture" and keep your eye on the goals and objectives of the business.

* Develop deliberate relationships with key people on every level.

* Keep your eyes and ears open.

* Acquire the skills to lead through mid-level managers.

* Be aware of the impact of your communication with others.

* Keep your team engaged.

* Control what you can and influence when you cannot.

* Run interference for your team when possible.

* Be disciplined and focused with your time and that of your team's time.

* Find a way to balance work and personal life.

Build on your foundation

Think through who will be impacted by you in your new

role (new boss, peers, colleagues, team) and prepare for initial conversations with them. Seek guidance from others who have made this transition before you. Take advice on potential pitfalls.

+ Take risks, manage uncertainty, appear calm.

+ "Walk the Talk." Behave the way you expect others to behave.

+ Know when and how to push back.

+ Tackle difficult communication issues head on with the support of a boss, HR person, mentor, or coach.

+ Reinforce each person's value, and let them know how they are doing.

• Possess an inner strength and resolve, and be true to yourself.

+ Be open to listening and learning.

+ Be true to your values.

+ Pick your battles and know when to take a stand.

The Challenge

Being in any new role is anxiety producing in and of itself. Add to that the layer of complexity of a senior management role, and you may begin to question your capabilities. You may be worried about failure and may be asking yourself if you really have what it takes to succeed.

New leadership roles are exciting and rewarding but they can't be done without the support of a trusted confidante and sounding board.

Have the courage to ask the following questions:

+ Am I demonstrating leadership and confidence?

+ Am I able to influence others?

+ Will I have the impact I want?

+ Will I be able to meet the expectations of stakeholders, customers and employees?

+ How am I managing the competing demands of work and home?

By asking yourself these questions, you are opening yourself to personal growth and development. Don't be surprised when the answers to these questions help to reinforce your strengths and capabilities and your potential for greater success.

ABOUT THE AUTHOR

Kathleen Greer is founder and president of KGA, Inc., a human resources consulting firm based in Framingham, Massachusetts. Since 1982, KGA has been helping managers, employees, and organizations to become more healthy, productive, and profitable through the delivery of Employee Assistance Programs and other HR solutions such as training, coaching, consulting, and wellness. Kathleen brings a unique background in counseling and business to KGA and resides in Duxbury, Massachusetts with her husband.

Made in the USA
Charleston, SC
27 October 2012